THERE'S SOMETHING SPECIAL ABOUT CRANES

THERE'S SOMETHING SPECIAL ABOUT CRANES

Memories and Anecdotes about the fifteen species of Crane

by

George Archibald

Illustrated by

Julia Whatley

MOUNT ORLEANS PRESS

PREFACE

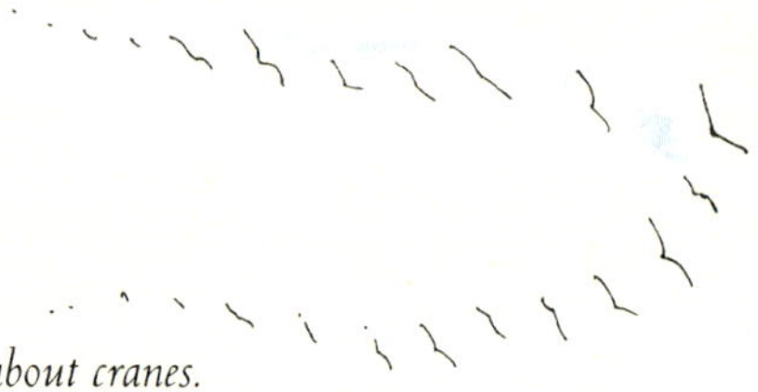

There's something special about cranes.
This book, beautifully illustrated by Julia Whatley, contains a true little story by George Archibald about each of the 15 species of cranes.

George's fascination with cranes began as an eight year old boy in 1954. At his one room school in rural Nova Scotia, Canada, his class used to listen

PREFACE

to a weekly radio program about science. One was a drama about a pair of Whooping Cranes, the female of which was terror stricken when her nest was discovered by a human flying low in a bush plane. Her mate comforted her that humans now wanted to help them. Since hearing that radio drama George was captivated by cranes.

The Whooping Crane of North America is the rarest of the 15 species of cranes. However crane conservation crosses borders: it is today an international enterprise, active in many countries.

At the age of 27 in Wisconsin, USA, George Archibald co-founded an organization dedicated to the conservation of cranes worldwide, the International Crane Foundation (ICF). Through ICF he continues to follow and help these magnificent birds.

BLACK CROWNED CRANES

first scientist to make a comprehensive study of these beautiful birds.

Like all cranes, Black Crowned Cranes form pairs. They select a wetland in which to build their platform nests for their two or three eggs. For 30 days, the pair take turns protecting and incubating their eggs.

Ethiopia is on a high altitude plateau just south of Egypt in northeast Africa. Lake Tana, the source of the Blue Nile river lies at the northern end of the Ethiopian Plateau. The wetlands that border Lake Tana are home to a famous bird, the Black Crowned Crane.

The Black Crowned Crane is native to wetlands from west Africa to Ethiopia and is the National Bird of Nigeria. Dr Shimelis Aynalem, from Ethiopia, is the

BLACK CROWNED CRANES

Shimelis wanted to learn more about their nests. Wearing waterproof waders that came up to his waist, he approached a nest. The water became deeper and deeper until it was almost impossible for Shimelis to walk. The nest was floating high above the muddy bottom of the wetland.

Eventually he found his feet had stuck fast in the mud: fortunately a fisherman heard his cries and came to his aid in a boat. Shimelis concluded that cranes sometimes build their nests in deep water where it is safe from land-roaming predators such a lions, leopards, hyenas and even humans.

BLACK-NECKED CRANES

BLACK-NECKED CRANES

The Black-necked Crane, a native of the Tibetan Plateau, is revered by the people of Tibet as a sacred bird. Their beauty, their grace, and the devotion within a family, does not go unnoticed. The cranes are strictly protected and can often be seen in the fields close to the Tibetan people. Once, when I stopped our vehicle to count the cranes, the Tibetans chased them off, fearing we might harm them. Another day, when I asked a herder why the cranes are sacred, he replied with complete confidence, 'Because they *are* sacred!' Enough said.

BLUE CRANES

One evening in a green pastured valley of South Africa, I observed a pair of Blue Cranes with their two small colts, who had come to spend in the night in the backwaters of a small pond created by a short dike. Several boys and their barking dogs suddenly appeared at the top of the far hill and proceeded to walk directly toward the dike. As they approached the dogs ran around the pond and straight into the family of cranes. It was getting dark and in the twilight impossible to see what happened. I imagined the worst amidst the commotion of barking dogs and loud calls of cranes. Suddenly, one crane swam across the pond flapping its wings on the water with dogs following several feet behind. Upon reaching the dike, the crane flew perhaps 50 meters to the pasture below

BLUE CRANES

was higher pitched than its mate, suggesting that the female had distracted the dogs while the male guarded the chicks. But had the chicks survived? The next morning at dawn I was there, and so was the family of four.

and ran in wide circles with head down and wings extended as if wounded. The dogs leaped from the dike in pursuit. As they approached, the crane flew another short distance and repeated its display. This ritual was repeated several times until the dogs gave up. Then there was darkness and silence. After some time, I heard a crane call from the hilltop area from which the boys and dogs had come. It was answered by a call from the pond. The voice of the hilltop bird

THE BROLGA

The Brolga, formerly known as the 'native companion' is also part of the crane family and is the Australian crane. My aboriginal guide, Roy Beasley, had extraordinary eyesight and survival skills. I had hired him to help me find the nests of Brolgas and Sarus cranes in the wilderness of the outback in northeastern Australia during the wet season.

The Brolga is easily confused with the Sarus, the Asian crane; both have red head colouring. The difference is the red on the Sarus extends further down the neck compared to the Brolga.

The landscape was flat with scattered trees and wetlands, and tall grasses that made it difficult to see cranes at all. Every once in a while a red head would

THE BROLGA

appear above the grasses. Roy's ability to spot that red head far exceeded mine. And when he spotted one, he would stand motionless with his back to a tree facing the direction of the crane. He claimed he was invisible to the crane as long as he didn't move. I followed his lead. To my amazement it worked. Between bouts of feeding, the red head would appear. Eventually that bird would return to the nest to swap with its mate who incubated the eggs in a cloud of blood drinking insects. When the incubating crane stood on the platform nest, it became obvious above the top of the grass. Sometime the nest would be quite near our points of motionless standing. Roy was a great teacher.

DEMOISELLE CRANES

Although the Demoiselles are the smallest of the cranes they have perhaps the most remarkable migration. In the autumn the demoiselles from the Mongolian plains migrate southwest across the Tibetan plateau scaling the Himalayas of Nepal before reaching their wintering grounds in Northwest India.

DEMOISELLE CRANES

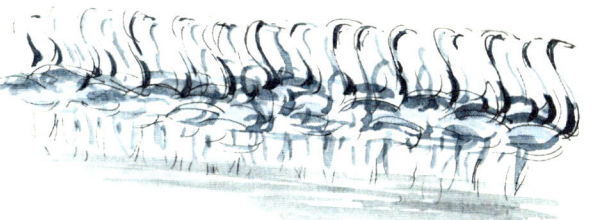

Here in the small village of Khichan in Rajasthan they must to be fed by the locals as part of the traditional custom. They then, restored, set off again in the spring in an onward direction. They avoid the late winter of the high Himalayas at 25,000 feet and veer northwestward to cross the Hindu Kush of Pakistan and Afghanistan (a mere 15,000 feet), to continue north to the steppes of Kazakhstan.

They then head east to their breeding grounds. Their migration is a clockwise movement over at least eight nations. Other migratory cranes follow a similar path too in the autumn and spring.

EURASIAN CRANES

Bernard Wessling studied Eurasian Cranes that nested near Hamburg, Germany. One pair with two chicks fed in a meadow they shared with a flock of Greylag Geese that included many goslings. Each day a fox took one of the goslings. Although the geese were upset by the fox, they continued to feed on the meadow.

EURASIAN CRANES

The cranes ignored the fox until one of their chicks was taken. Their response was to drive the geese from the meadow. Left alone with their single colt, there was little to attract the fox. His story demonstrates a level of intelligence in cranes.

GREY CROWNED CRANES

The habitat of the Grey Crowned Crane has an enormous range stretching from east to southern Africa. It is the National Bird of Uganda and even featured on the flag.

Jimmy Muheebwa is a Ugandan farmer who loves Grey Crowned Cranes. Although the cranes are protected, the wetlands in which they nest and rear their young are rapidly disappearing as the growing population of humans needs more farmland.

GREY CROWNED CRANES

Jimmy works with the farmers to promote wetland conservation and restoration. In one valley where the wetland was drained, the local people soon did not have water. The former wetland had acted like a huge sponge to absorb water during the rainy season and slowly release it during the dry season. The farmers did not know that.

By stopping the farming and blocking the escape of water by planting wetland plants, the wetlands were soon restored providing plenty of water both for the cranes and the local people.

Jimmy also helped the farmers secure bees, goats, pigs and chickens to improve their livelihoods. In return, he asked them to protect the cranes and the wetlands.

HOODED CRANES

HOODED CRANES

In a rice paddy in a narrow valley of Kyushu Island, Japan, there is a roosting place of a flock of about one hundred Hooded Cranes. During the day, the cranes fed far from this valley, but in late afternoon, they returned to a grass hillside with a commanding views high above the roosting area. Here they preened, rested, displayed and made lots of noise. After the sun had disappeared and it was almost dark, the cranes silently glided to the flooded rice paddy where in continued silence they perhaps remained for the remainder of the night. It appeared that the pre-roosting area was for social facilitation, while the silence at the roost was an adaptation to avoid attracting predators.

RED CROWNED CRANES

In 1977 I accompanied my Korean colleagues to search for wintering Red-crowned Cranes in the Demilitarized Zone that divides North and South Korea. We travelled from army post to army post and were encouraged when a soldier in the central highlands was able to report sightings. As we entered the Cheorwon Basin the weather was foggy and extremely cold. From the top of a high brush-covered hill surrounded by wide expanses of frozen rice fields,

RED CROWNED CRANES

we peered through telescopes into the fog. When I first spotted a white spot, I thought it was a piece of frost-covered plastic. Then it moved! That morning we counted 125 Red-crowned Cranes. Subsequently, the population has increased to almost 1000.

SANDHILL CRANES

My wife and I kept an injured male crane whom we named Sandy. He spent the winter with our chickens and was remarkably tame. In the spring he was released and moved from the barn to the wetland near our home. Sometimes a pair of wild cranes landed, and they chased Sandy. We feared for his welfare. But the wild cranes never stayed very long. One day a family of cranes, a pair with their juvenile, also landed near Sandy. They spent the night beside him roosting in the wetland. In early morning the family departed to feed elsewhere. But they returned in late afternoon and joined Sandy. This routine continued for several days.

Then the pair departed leaving their juvenile with Sandy. The two were inseparable. Every day, they came near our home to feed at a spot where I placed some corn.

SANDHILL CRANES

One day I forgot to feed the cranes. They approached the house, walked up the steps to the front porch and stood calling near the kitchen door. We got the message and soon gave them more corn. Eventually, the newly-paired cranes started dueting together. The day the deer hunting season started, Sandy disappeared perhaps killed through mistaken identity. The lone female called and called for several days and then disappeared. The following spring a lone female crane returned and called and called. Eventually she departed and silence returned. We were lucky to have lived even for a season with Sandy and his mate before this tragedy.

THE SARUS CRANE

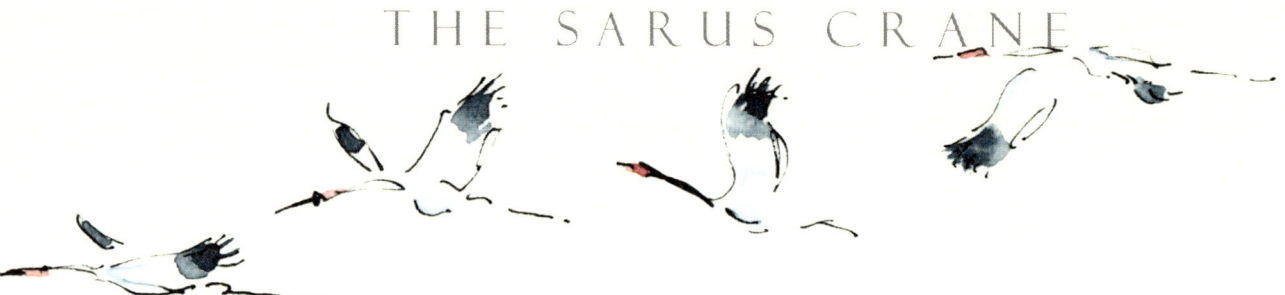

During the dry season hundreds of Sarus used to gather at the Tram Chim (bird swamp) wetland on the Mekong Delta of Vietnam. When water levels were low, they fed in dry areas where aquatic plants survived by creating tubers, a prime food of cranes. During the hottest time of day, the cranes flew to wetlands to bath, drink, display and loaf. By

THE SARUS CRANE

placing myself on a dike along the flight path between the feeding area and the loafing area, I was able to photograph the cranes. One afternoon during a period of perhaps one hour, I counted 646 flying low overhead in small groups. It was a great thrill to be so close to the world's tallest bird that flies.

SIBERIAN CRANES

How can six eggs that are about to hatch, survive a 10,000 mile journey from the tundra of Siberia to an incubator in Madison, Wisconsin?

When Dr Vladimir Flint collected each egg from its nest, he slid it into a soft woollen sock. With eggs hanging he carried them to a gigantic helicopter that hovered nearby. Next the eggs were placed in a small insulated and carefully padded suitcase, warmed with hot water bottles. The helicopter landed in an airport in Chorkodah and soon Flint and his precious cargo were aboard a commercial flight, 5000 miles west to Moscow to meet Ron Sauey from ICF. Carrying a second suitcase with the required interior, Ron received the eggs, and with a huge hug bade farewell to Flint and continued the amazing passage of the

SIBERIAN CRANES

eggs towards the west. Their export across the Iron Curtain during the Cold War was preceded by three years of negotiations and many permits. Ron's huge files, the work of three years applying for permits, were not even examined by either Russian or US officials. When Ron and his eggs stopped in Gander, Canada to change planes, he encountered Frank Sinatra and his entourage headed east. As he added hot water to the bottles, he was alarmed to hear peeping in the suitcase. One of the eggs had started to hatch. Opening the suitcase to check things while flying over Cleveland, Ohio, Ron was thrilled to meet a crane chick. He named it Aeroflot. During the next week, the remaining eggs all hatched. They were added to a small group of Siberian Cranes at the International Crane Foundation – a safeguard against extinction of a species in decline.

WATTLED CRANES

Wattled Cranes are known for their silence. They seldom call, in sharp contrast to other crane species that are quite noisy. Perhaps the most dramatic call of cranes is the unison call, a complicated duet at highest volume usually performed by mated pairs. The unison call appears to have two functions: sex and threat. It helps in the formation of pair bonding and thus perhaps encourages hormonal synchronization of pairs. It signals their aggression to other cranes

WATTLED CRANES

threatening to invade a pair's space. I discovered during my studies of captive Wattled Cranes that they do have a unison call but it is usually performed in the dead of the night. Years later, I had a chance to camp beside a roosting area of about 130 Wattled Cranes in Ethiopia. The silent cranes arrived at the shallow waters of the roost at dusk. To my surprise, between approximately two and five a.m. many pairs commenced their screech-like unison calls. My Ethiopian colleague, Hadis Tadale, who had studied Wattled Cranes for several years, had never heard this display: he was amazed. So what is the function of the Wattled Crane's unison call? Although it was pitch dark and thus impossible to see the cranes, there was utter silence but for the unison calls. It is likely they were not threatening one another. Perhaps the duet was a way of saying in the darkness, "I'm here and I love you".

WHITE-NAPED CRANES

Mongolia is a stronghold for the White-naped Crane. It's also the home of a remarkable man, Mr Batsukh Galsan – the CEO of the mining company Rio Tinto, and former ambassador to Canada, China and Ambassador at Large for Mongolia's Ministry of Foreign Affairs and Trade. Batsukh's hobby is wildlife photography.

My colleague Dr Nyambayar Batbayar and I discovered a nest of a White-naped Cranes near the road in a small wetland about an hour's drive from Batsukh's office in

WHITE-NAPED CRANES

Ulaanbaatar. We informed Batsukh of an amazing opportunity for pictures. I had to leave Mongolia too soon to see his photographs but I received them later by email. One photo of the cranes in their nest was extraordinary. A White-naped Crane was sitting on its nest and behind it stood three white cranes – Siberians. Batsukh's comment was 'Here are white cranes near the nest.' Little did he realize that the Siberian Crane is a very rare bird in Mongolia. His picture is historic.

WHOOPING CRANES

WHOOPING CRANES

A pair of Whooping Cranes were being watched in the wild in Wisconsin for several spring breeding seasons; they had only laid infertile eggs. Something was wrong. Sara Zimorski, a researcher at ICF, substituted a fertile egg prduced into captivity into the nest of this infertile pair. The egg hatched and the chick was reared. The following year, Sara planned to repeat the protocol. While walking through deep water as she approached the nest, she heard peeping. Standing on the nest was a newly-hatched chick. The pair had produced a fertile egg. Sara was happy to return her egg to the incubator at ICF.

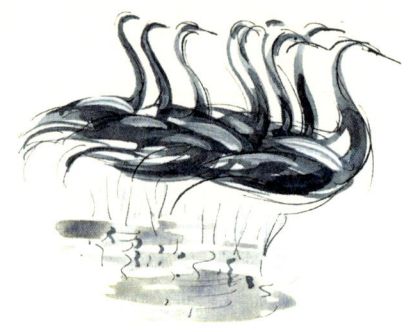

Edited by Mirabel Helme

First published in 2018 by The International Crane Foundation
© 2018 The International Crane Foundation
This edition published by Mount Orleans Press 2019
https://anthonyeyre.com

All rights reserved. No part of this publication may be reproduced,
stored in a retrieval system, or transmitted in any form or by any means,
electronic, mechanical, photocopying or otherwise, without
the prior permission of the copyright holder.

CIP data for this title are available from the British Library

Typography and book production by Anthony Eyre

ISBN 978-1-912945-01-6

Printed in Poland